CALLED TO AFRICA

A Mini-Guide for Your First Mission Trip to Uganda

K. S. Laster

Called To Africa Copyright ©2017 Live in Light Ministries. All Rights Reserved.

All rights reserved. No part of this book may be reproduced in any form or by any electronic or mechanical means including information storage and retrieval systems, without permission in writing from the author. The only exceptions are for the purpose of copying check lists, sample materials or by a reviewer, who may quote short excerpts in a review.

Cover designed by Cover Designer

Printed in the United States of America

First Printing: Dec 2017
Live in Light Ministries
a DBA of Share the Lovies Inc.
www.liveinlightministries.org

ISBN-9781976774393

In memory of my dad, who taught me that the mission field begins at home and extends to all of God's creatures; and Gilbert, who showed me on a daily basis that the mission field includes the work place.

CONTENTS

The Call to Mission in Uganda 1
Brief History Since Independence 7
About Uganda: Culture, Geography and Demographics 15
Booking Flights and Air Travel 23
Planning and Preparation 35
Packing and Gift Items 43
Health and Safety 57
Arrival and Transportation 67
Food and Lodging 76
Communicating with Friends and Family in the States 84
Communicating in Uganda 88
All About Flexibility and Patience 97
Free Time, To Safari or Not to Safari 100
Rewinding, Reflecting and Returning Home 110

Chapter 1

THE CALL TO MISSION IN UGANDA

Isaiah 6:8 (NIV)
Then I heard the voice of the Lord, saying, "Whom should I send? Who will go for us?" Then I said, "Here am I. Send me!"

If you are reading this, then I assume that you have been called, or are at least seriously considering a call, to serve in Uganda. Consider yourself blessed by the Lord, as you are about to embark (or are seriously considering embarking) on a journey that will reach into the deepest parts of your heart and soul. I am 100% certain that if you follow God's lead to serve the poor and orphans in Uganda, your life will be changed forever. With that, let me be the first to welcome you (in advance) to Uganda!

It is good news that God did not give you a spirit of timidity (2 Tim 1:7) as your assignment is not for the faint of heart, however, if you are a bit uncertain about what lies ahead, be encouraged and excited as God's gracious favor, along with planning and preparation, will help ensure a successful mission. If you are a highlighter, go ahead and mark this next statement, *a Spirit filled mission trip to Uganda will result in an experience from which you will leave feeling more contented, rewarded and yes, possibly exhausted than you could ever imagine.*

It is likely that many of you are reading a downloaded sample so you can determine whether this guide is worth investing your time and money. I do the exact same thing before I purchase an online book. Usually, I can make a good judgment by reading the first few pages provided in the free sample. Occasionally, the sample is too short. In those situations, unfortunately, I sometimes figure out after reading a few more pages of the purchased version that the book really does not provide what I was looking for and that I have unwittingly misspent some of my self-imposed e-book budget. To avoid any unnecessary frustration, I want to be clear, before we get into the more exciting mission planning and preparation suggestions, what this mini-book *Is and Is Not* intended to be.

First and foremost, God suggested that I use the materials that I had compiled for a recent team mission trip to Uganda to help others. He proposed that the materials could be turned into a planning guide for those He has called to travel for their first mission trip to Africa and Uganda specifically. I should add that God made the suggestion in January, as we were talking about the plans He had for us to focus on in the upcoming year. Candidly, at the time, I was not very excited about the idea and thought I had enough on my plate since it was only a couple of months before my husband and I would be making our fourth sortie to Uganda while leading a mission team for the first time. There was still a lot of prep work to be completed before the journey. Ever the negotiator, I agreed to focus on converting the mission information into a booklet after the March mission trip and promised that it would be completed by the end of the year.

"March Mission: Uganda" was a huge success. Every one of our thirteen-member team (self-included) had an amazing experience. Every team member now (if they didn't already) has a heart for Uganda and its people. None of our team members was ready to leave Uganda at the end of our visit and everyone wants to return in the future. Ugandan lives were changed. American lives were changed. Ugandans were blessed, and Americans were blessed even more. God's glory shown. I would love to hear your stories after you experience it for yourself, as I truly believe that you will know exactly what I mean. (If you are so inclined to share them, please email me at info@liveinlightministries.org.)

After returning from Uganda, God waited a few weeks before reminding me of our discussion about turning the mission planning materials into a guidebook. Somehow, though, I was even busier than before the March trip with a new business that was really taking off, summer sports activities, a mission scouting trip to Central America and all the other things that can consume my (and possibly your?) time. I pushed work on the "mini guide" off again, and reiterated the promise to complete it by the end of the year. After a very full summer, here we are in late, late August. Work is just as busy. Instead of summer sports, the focus is a new school year, fall sports activities and new bible study groups. But time keeps on ticking...and with the grace of God and commitment to my commitment, the booklet will be ready for someone planning their first trip after the first of the year. (If you are the person using it to help plan your trip in 2018, please send me a note at the email address above, as I've often wondered and prayed about your upcoming journey.)

So, back to what this booklet *Is and Is Not* intended to be:

IS: As mentioned above, this mini-book is a planning guide, based on what my family has learned from our previous four and upcoming fifth trips to Uganda. It is intended to be a helpful tool for first time mission trippers to Uganda seeking pre-trip information related to booking, planning, packing, traveling, eating and doing. It does include some anecdotal experiences from previous mission trips to Uganda and a few suggestions as to some interesting and fun excursions if you have some free time during your time in the country.

IS NOT: This mini-book is not intended to be an exhaustive or detailed resource for those who have traveled previously to Uganda or even Africa. Although an overview is provided, it does not include extensive details about the rich and sometimes tragic history of Uganda, as several great resources already exist. While the mini-guide may not comprise everything one might possibly want to know before traveling to Uganda, it is my hope that it shares enough information to convince you to take the next step. By following God's call, you will begin a journey of your own amazing, life altering experiences thereby answering any remaining questions.

Chapter 2

BRIEF HISTORY SINCE INDEPENDENCE

1 Chronicles 16:24 (RSV)
"Declare his glory among the nations, His marvelous works among all the peoples!"

In his early career in journalism and as a young Member of Parliament, Winston Churchill traveled to Africa on several occasions. In *My African Journey* (1908), he captured the splendor of Uganda with the following description:

"The kingdom of Uganda is a fairy-tale. You climb up ... and at the end there is a wonderful new world. The scenery is *and, most of all, the people are different from anything elsewhere to be seen in the whole range of Africa ... I say: 'Concentrate on Uganda'. For magnificence, for variety of form and colour, for profusion of brilliant life – bird, insect, reptile, beast – for vast scale — Uganda is truly the pearl of Africa."*[2]

The young Mr. Churchill summed it up very well. Uganda and its people are truly beautiful.

For those interested in knowing more about the country to which you have been called on mission, there are several very good resources regarding Uganda's sometimes-turbulent recent history. Many books and articles have reconfirmed my calling to serve a nation that has suffered at the hands of ruthless warlords and unconscionable despots who sought to promote personal interests to the detriment of the country and its people. Rather than repeat those more detailed works, the summary below shares some of the challenges experienced by Ugandans since achieving independence from Great Britain on October 9th, 1962.

Toward the end the end of Britain's colonial rule, various partisan groups began positioning to assume power. Demonstrating political savvy, Milton Obote created the Uganda's National Congress political organization and aligned with the country's ruling party led by the Bagandan King. Obote's position and alliance helped him gain victory in the country's first election for Prime Minister in 1963. King Mutesa II, of the Bagandan ruling party was elected as Uganda's first President in the two-leader system. Following those elections, much of the country experienced a tumultuous and sometimes horrifying forty-year period of internal strife, wars and terror.

As Prime Minister, Obote found it difficult to bring the country together as many Ugandans sought to maintain pre-existing tribal allegiances, especially those associated with the King's ruling party who had the support of President Mutesa II. In order to exercise complete control, Obote relied upon the strength of his military organization, led by Major General Idi Amin, to overthrow the President in 1966. Shortly thereafter, Obote declared Uganda to be a single leader Republic, named himself President and abolished the traditional Ugandan Kingdoms.

Many historians report that the years following Obote's coup exemplified a repressive dictatorship that resulted in the destruction and demise of thousands of

Ugandans who supported opposing political parties. Obote's reign of misery and pain over the people of Uganda ended in 1971, when his leadership was usurped in a coup led by Major General Idi Amin, the commander of the Ugandan military. The period that followed was an eight-year reign of terror that was even more diabolical than Obote's years in office. Shortly after taking control, Amin caused wide spread destruction to the fragile Ugandan economy when he forced over 50,000 Asian business owners and workers to leave the country in 1972. Over the next seven years, Amin became increasingly paranoid and commanded mass killings of hundreds of thousands of Ugandans of Obote's ancestral heritage or believed to support his political views.

With dreams of even greater political dominion, in 1978 Amin unsuccessfully led his military forces in an attempt to invade Tanzania. Shortly thereafter, in April 1979, previously exiled Ugandan leaders and troops, who had garnered support from the Tanzanian government and army, successfully conquered the Amin regime. Following several transitional months of political competition and internal leadership clashes, Milton Obote once again emerged as the elected leader of Uganda despite questionable electoral results.

Unfortunately, in a repeat of his previous rule, Obote allowed his military leaders and forces to become more powerful than his ability to control.

By 1981, in part as response to the extreme cruelty and domination the military exercised throughout the country, Ugandan resistance groups began to form. One such group, the National Resistance Army (NRA) led by Yoweri Museveni, initiated a popular rebellion that escalated into a five-year civil war. Bitterly contested between Obote's government and the rebel fighters, the war affected much of the country. As many as one-half million people are believed to have lost their lives during this time.

One area of particular devastation occurred in the Luweero District, located north of Kampala, where Obote believed that rebel fighters were hiding with support from local villagers. Obote directed his forces to regain control of the district by eliminating everyone thought to be loyal to Museveni's cause. To carry out this direction, government forces offered civilians who claimed support for Obote the opportunity to move into internment camps under military control within the district. Unfortunately, the military commanders did not have the training or resources to provide adequate amounts of food, water or other necessities for the residents within the camps. Those held within the camps struggled to survive with limited food and severe mistreatment. Local citizens that refused to relocate to the Luweero internment camps faced even more dire circumstances. Considered loyal to the rebel cause, many suffered brutal elimination under Obote's direction. As a precautionary measure to ensure that the rebels were unable to find food or shelter, government forces robbed and destroyed virtually all of the houses and crops within the district.

The abuses that occurred in the Luweero district continue to be felt today. A large percentage of the adult male population was decimated during the five-year civil war. Unfortunately, the abuses upon girls and women were just as significant. Mercenary fighters, who joined Obote's military from other African countries, repeatedly raped and beat them. It is believed that these militants were the first to bring AIDS to the area and through it set a circular course of painful death and destruction in the Luweero communities for years to come.

After years of devastating internal fighting, Obote and his forces were overthrown and forced into exile for the second time. Yoweri Kaguat Museveni became the President of Uganda on January 29, 1986. While some allege that Museveni has unfairly influenced the presidential electoral process, he is frequently credited with the progress Uganda has achieved during his tenure. Successfully disposing of term limits in 2005, Museveni has been in power for over thirty years. His most recent electoral victory occurred in 2016, when he was elected for another five-year term.

During this time, the nation has benefited from strong alliances that Museveni developed with the United States and other westernized countries. In 2006, these allies helped the Ugandan troops push the Lord's Resistance Army, a rebel group commanded by Joseph Kony, out of Uganda. Before being forced out of the country, Kony and the LRA had maintained a vicious stronghold in the northern region, slaughtering and committing atrocities against thousands of men, women and children. His appalling practices over the previous twenty-year period included child slavery and forced marriages.

While its history reveals a journey of tears, Uganda has experienced a period of relative peace and commercial development over the last decade. Though currently on the United Nation's list of Least Developed Countries, there is much hope for Uganda's future. It is my belief that God will prosper Uganda through the seeds you will plant, the lives you will touch and the work for which God called you.

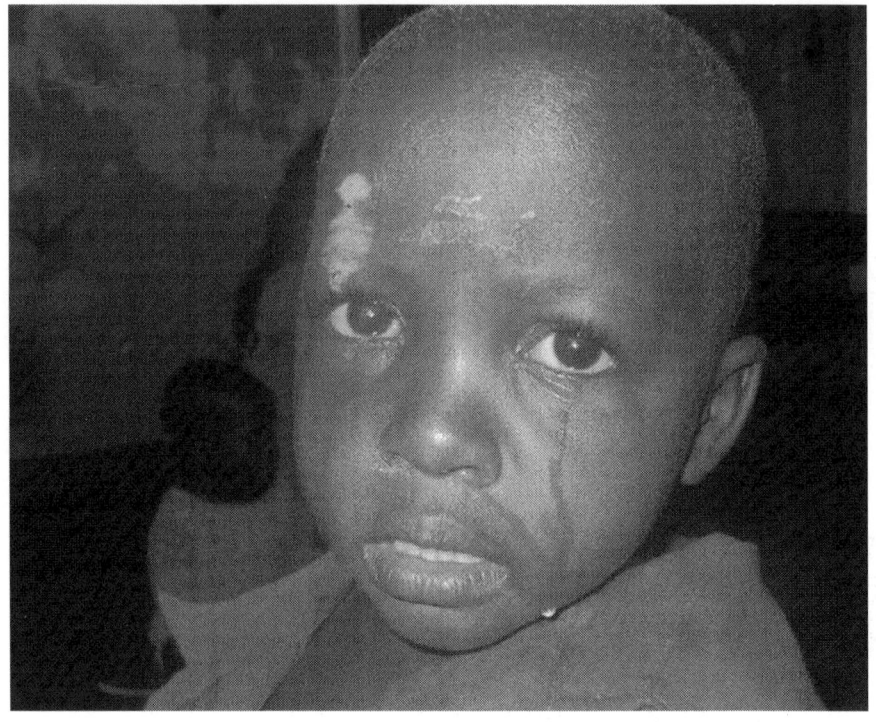

3

Chapter 3

ABOUT UGANDA: CULTURE, GEOGRAPHY AND DEMOGRAPHICS

Matthew 28:19-20 (NIV)
Therefore go and make disciples of all nations, baptizing them in the name of the Father and of the Son and of the Holy Spirit, and teaching them to obey everything I have commanded you. And surely I am with you always, to the very end of the age."

Uganda has an extremely diverse ethnic, religious, and political culture.

Geography

Located on the equator in sub-Saharan East Africa, its neighboring Countries include South Sudan to the north, Rwanda and Tanzania to the south, with Kenya and Congo to the east and west respectively. Uganda is a country of undeniable beauty, plentiful natural resources, amazing wildlife and lots and lots of wonderful people. My oldest daughter had the following to say in a blog post during our last mission trip to Uganda:

> *"For many of our team, it is their first time here in Uganda so being able to share this experience with them is amazing and exciting! The drive from the airport to the capital city of Kampala is where the first bit of culture shock occurs. And by this I mean the people... EVERYWHERE. To put it in a little better perspective, Uganda is smaller than the state of Nevada. Are you with me? BUT, get this... Uganda's population is 41 million, while Nevada's is less than three million. Are you following me here?! That is a LOT of people, in not a lot of space."*

Culture

After being abolished by Milton Obote in 1967, the traditional Ugandan kingdoms were reinstated by President Museveni in 1993 and are now protected under the 1995 Constitution. Today, most Ugandans culturally identify with one of the ancestral tribal kingdoms. The Buganda tribe is the largest ethnic group in the country representing almost twenty percent of the population. Each of the tribes expresses rich cultural differences through traditional dance, music, art and crafts. If you are interested in seeing and hearing some traditional performances, be sure to visit the Ndere Cultural Center for a dinner performance while you are in Kampala. The event provides an entertaining and informative evening that will be enjoyed by mission teams of all ages. Though we have been (more than once) it is always looked forward to for future trips.

Culturally, Ugandan men are more likely to travel from rural areas to other larger towns or cities in order to find employment. While the men are away working in the cities, the women remain in the rural villages and often shoulder the burden of providing for traditionally large families on a daily basis. They take care of children, often walk long distances to get water (sometimes twice daily), collect firewood, cook meals over open fires, work the gardens, raise livestock, if the family is fortunate to have animals, and may have a small side business selling or trading items with other villagers. These tasks make for a long, hard day and most of the women living in rural Uganda accomplish them each and every day without electricity or running water. In the urban areas, women continue to experience legal, economic and social constraints but are becoming increasingly more likely to work outside of the home, often in teaching, nursing, tourism or secretarial positions.

When meeting for the first time, men are more likely to approach and greet visitors. Women; however, often tend to be more reserved. This does not mean that they don't want to meet you. On the contrary, from my experience, most Ugandan women genuinely appreciate a visitor who makes the first friendly overture so do not hesitate to introduce yourself. Despite the initial shyness, women will greet you with enthusiasm and huge welcoming smiles on subsequent encounters.

There are children everywhere in Uganda. Whether male or female, they are typically not shy and are very interested in you. They want to smile, laugh skip, hop and play, with you. They want to do what you are doing, listen to what you are listening and watch what you are watching, especially if it is a video you took with your phone or camera of them smiling and laughing while playing with you. Don't be surprised when they call (or yell) Mzungu (white person) at you, repeatedly, and even though you know they know your name. They may ask, "How are you?" frequently, and gleefully anticipate your response of, "I am fine, how are you?" If you want to surprise them with some local flavor, respond with "Gyendi" (Jen-dee), to say 'I am fine', followed by, "Olyotia" (O-lee-o-tee-yah) asking 'How are you?" Be prepared for that exchange to result in surprised laughter. No matter how much they appreciate your attempts to speak in their local language, and regardless of how well you say it, Ugandan children love to laugh at the way Luganda sounds from our American tongues.

Be sure to take a couple of extra arms and hands with you because Ugandan children will want to hold your hand and walk with you even if they do not know where you are going. Some (okay, most) will climb (or try to climb) into your lap if you are sitting down. If you have blond hairs on your arm (like my husband) they will be fascinated and playfully tug on them....over and over again while laughing at your exaggerated pained expression. They love to sing songs and play games. The hardest I have ever seen a group of children (from any country) laugh was when playing Red Rover with my daughters who were then 15 and 19. In my (somewhat biased) opinion, they are the most joyful, loving children I have ever been blessed to meet.

Religion

Religion plays an important role in daily Ugandan life. Approximately 85% of the population identifies as Christians while 14% adheres to Islam. Traditional indigenous rituals and beliefs, however, continue to have a stronghold. In a 2010 survey, over one-fourth of the respondents reported a belief that sacrifices made to ancestors or spirits could protect them from harm.[6]

Life Expectancy

The Ugandan people are benefitting from the last decade of civil peace and increased assistance from the outside world. According to the World Health Organization (WHO), the average life expectancy for Ugandans has increased from 58 years to 62 years.[7] Despite this increase in life expectancy, Uganda has the second youngest population in the world with 55% of its population being under the age of 18.[8]

Weather

If you enjoy constant, comfortable warmth, then Uganda is the place for you. The equatorial temperature of Uganda is nearly perfect (at least in my opinion).

Daytime is usually warm between 70 to 90 degrees. With the average annual temperature being around 78 degrees, there is rarely a need to put on long sleeves. While the temperature is unlikely to drop below 60 degrees even at night, it is best to be safe by packing a sweater or hoodie just in case one of those rare events occurs or if you are traveling into the mountains. Uganda traditionally has two rainy seasons, March through May and October through November. However, these seasons can be very unpredictable. One of our previous trips was during the third week of March and we only experienced spotty rain showers during a couple of the nights while we were sleeping. On another of our trips in late July, it rained almost all day, every day for three days straight while we were in Kampala. The dirt roads in the city were a muddy mess.

TIP: Be sure to pack a plastic rain poncho even if you will not be traveling during one of the traditional rainy seasons.

Chapter 4

BOOKING FLIGHTS AND AIR TRAVEL

Mark 16:15 (NIV)
"He said to them, "You are to go to all the world and preach the Good News to every person."

Booking your flight and other travel arrangements is one of the most important and expensive steps of your pre-trip planning process. Prices to Uganda from the United States (and Europe) vary widely depending upon the time of year in which you will be traveling, how far in advance you book your tickets and your flexibility with respect to your specific departure date, flight itinerary and layover destinations. Our previous four trips have varied greatly in cost for each round trip ticket. The lowest ticket price was for a trip made in March while the other three were for July departures with return dates in July or early August. Tickets for each of the trips were purchased between three and four months in advance of the departure dates.

Based on research of travel dates and ticket prices for the last few years, July is typically the most expensive month to travel, followed by late December. Importantly, if you are able to lock down your trip dates and purchase your airline tickets with a longer lead-time, you can find better prices. For an upcoming trip, we were able to book our tickets for a July departure for just $1200 each, the lowest price we have ever paid. The difference seems to be that the recent purchase occurred seven months in advance of the trip. Another international traveler shared that tickets for travel to Uganda seem to be a bit lower around Black Friday and Cyber Monday in November. I can't confirm whether this is true but anecdotally, both the $1200 ticket price for the upcoming trip in July and the ticket for the March trip were purchased in that November time frame.

TIP: Late November seems to be a good time to purchase tickets for spring and summer travel to Uganda.

If getting the lowest ticket price possible is important to you, then it also pays if you can be flexible with your departure date. Delaying your departure by a day or two or leaving one or two days earlier can have a significant impact on the cost of your ticket. For example, the tickets for our next trip would have cost several hundred dollars more if we had departed one day earlier or later. A good way to check prices over a thirty-day period is by using the Matrix ITA software, a free service offered by Google at http://matrix.itasoftware.com/. ITA will show you available ticket prices for most major airlines over a thirty-day period as long as you click the box indicating that your travel dates are flexible. It's also important to make sure to select the number of travelers for whom you need to purchase tickets if you are traveling as a group. I made a mistake recently and searched with the single traveler default option selected, only to be disappointed when the $900 ticket I found for our normal travel route was not available for a larger group.

Unfortunately, you cannot purchase tickets through the ITA website. After identifying the tickets that you would like to purchase, you can provide the desired itinerary to a travel agent who should be able to find them for the same price. I typically copy and paste the travel details and the information that ITA includes at the bottom that says "helpful for travel agent" and email it to my preferred agent. Using this method, my travel agents have been able to find the same schedule and fare. Occasionally, they have been able to add another small promotional discount that the airline is offering travel agents for directing customers to the airline. If you prefer to purchase directly from the airline, that will also work. I have usually been able to find the same travel schedule and price on the airline's website by searching the exact travel dates as the preferred route found through the ITA program.

TIP: Find your preferred flights and the best available prices over a thirty day period through the Matrix ITA software offered by Google.

Flexibility, with respect to your originating airport, and your choice of layover airport are also important considerations. A very nice regional airport is located very close to where we live; however, international ticket prices departing and returning to it are much higher than national or international airports. Tickets purchased for departures from larger airports are often up to $500 less per ticket if we are willing to drive between three and five hours to a larger departure airport. The choice of connecting airports will also affect the price of the ticket. Promotions are often offered for connecting flights through Dubai on Emirates, or through DOHA on Qatar Airways, if you are open to a longer than normal layover, often between twelve to twenty-four hours. Both airports have hotels if you want to relax and both countries allow free short term visas for visitors from the US and Europe if you want to take some time to tour the local area (hop-on-hop-off bus tours are offered in both cities with very good reviews on Trip Advisor). Check the airline websites for more information about getting visas after you arrive at the airport. Friends who have flown with these airlines report that they very much enjoyed the flights and some say they prefer these airlines for travel to Africa.

If you have a limited number of days for your mission trip, you may want to choose a route that provides shorter layovers. We have flown through Brussels,

Belgium, Amsterdam and London Heathrow, all of which were perfectly fine. Of the three, Brussels Airport was probably the easiest to navigate. Typically, shorter layovers are preferred over longer layovers, but not too short. We had a ninety-minute layover on one of our journeys and that felt a bit too stressful and rushed. Two and one-half to three hours seems to work well; however, if you end up with a layover longer than five or six hours, check online before your trip to see what options are available at the airport for renting a sleeping room with shower facilities for a few hours. A shower and a few hours rest can make all the difference in how you feel while on a twenty-four hour plus travel schedule.

Even with a break and shower, travel to Africa from the U.S. is a long haul and jet lag can be a bear. Regardless of the route and layover schedule you choose, based on experience with international travel, adjustment in the destination country seems to go much better if you arrive in the evening or night if you can make it to your hotel or guesthouse at a reasonable hour, preferably before midnight. The important thing is to get a good night's sleep so you can wake up fresh in the morning ready to experience an amazing country for the first time. If needed, a late afternoon arrival time would probably be okay but I strongly advise against an early morning arrival. It can be miserable trying to stay awake for an entire day after a long travel schedule.

TIP: Schedule an evening arrival time if at all possible so you can focus on adjusting to the time difference with a good night's sleep.

We have found it helpful to begin adjusting our waking and sleeping schedule before we leave the U.S. so we can have an easier transition to Africa time and (hopefully) reduce the impacts of jet lag. Depending on the time of year and where you live in the States, be prepared for a seven to eleven hour time difference. Part of our pre-flight plan includes staying up late the night before we depart with the hope of making it easier to sleep on the first international flight to our connecting airport. For some of you, the Ambien that your international travel doctor suggested may come in very handy, I refused it our first three trips but tried one-half of a pill on our last trip. The Ambien really helped and I did not experience much grogginess upon waking.

For the second international leg of the trip, we have found it extremely beneficial to stay awake the entire flight to Uganda so that it is easier to sleep for several hours after our evening arrival in Uganda. You will probably need to test some schedules to find what works for you. Notably, we followed this schedule on our first two trips and had almost no issues adjusting to the time change upon arrival. As experienced travelers on our third trip, we chose not to follow the plan and stayed awake on the first international leg but slept on the second international flight to Uganda. What followed was by far the worst night we have ever experienced in Uganda. Lying miserably wide-awake in our beds until finally drifting off an hour or so before it was time to get up for our first day on mission, we then went through our entire first day of mission battling the worst case of jet lag ever. Not surprisingly, on our fourth trip we reverted to the "flight sleep plan" (and incorporated one-half of an Ambien pill for the first international flight) to make sure we did not relive the prior experience.

TIP: Consider adjusting your sleep patterns closer to Africa time by staying up late the night before your departure so you can sleep on the first international flight and stay awake on the second.

Sometimes, future travelers ask whether a short-term missionary to Uganda should purchase travel insurance. As with any insurance product, the answer varies for each person. If you are concerned about purchasing tickets several months in advance, insurance may provide some comfort. Just be sure to read the fine print and understand exactly what you are buying. After reading the details of an offered policy, I realized that the person attempting to sell me the travel insurance was even confused about the coverage provisions of a trip protection policy. To be safe, double check by thoroughly reading before purchasing to make sure that the potential risk or event you are trying to insure against is covered.

Importantly, some credit cards provide the same or similar travel protection coverage at no additional charge if you use the card to purchase the tickets. Again, be sure to read the details to understand exactly what coverage is provided. I recently compared two highly advertised cards that focus on rewarding purchases with travel mileage benefits. One of the cards, Capitol One Venture card, did not include travel cancellation or interruption benefits. The Citibank American Advantage card; however, offered free travel cancellation and interruption coverage that was almost identical to the insurance policy that was available for purchase from the airline or travel agent. Since credit card companies may change card terms or benefits at any time, be sure to check your cards before you buy an airline ticket or before you select a new credit card if this benefit is important to you.

TIP: Some credit cards provide travel cancellation and interruption coverage for airline tickets purchased with the card.

Last, but certainly not least, for consideration when booking flights is where to sit. Unless, you are able to afford business class or better seats, the airline policy regarding seating may be of extreme importance to you. Since we usually have at least four travelers in our group, our preferred airlines allow travelers to visit their website immediately after purchasing tickets to view the cabin layout and select specific economy rows and seats. If you are unsure which seats to avoid on a specific flight or plane, visit seatguru.com to get valuable seating information about all of the seats in the cabin for your specific flight. By checking seat guru on a recent trip, we avoided selecting a row that looked ideal. Due to airline modifications to the plane; however, the row we were considering actually had less legroom than any other row in the economy cabin. Notably, on our last trip to Uganda, one of our travel legs was on KLM. Unless the rules have changed recently, KLM requires travelers to pay a fee to select specific seats within the economy cabin up until 3 days prior to departure when they open up seat selection for all travelers. This rule was a bit stressful when trying to organize for a group of thirteen, the majority of whom had never been out of the country. As a result, we are avoiding group travel with KLM as much as possible.

The BIG TIP for this section; however, is to check with the airline before you purchase your ticket to see if it is possible, either at the time you buy your ticket or immediately afterwards by visiting the airline website, to purchase an exit row seat or a seat in the first row of the cabin that provides extra legroom. Many of the U.S. based airlines provide this option for a reasonable fee. We have also taken advantage of this option on both Brussels Air and KLM at very fair prices. Unfortunately, as noted above with respect to KLM, you will be unable to select seats in adjacent rows for others in your party until three days prior to departure.

TIP: Check with the airline before you purchase your ticket to see if it is possible, either at the time you buy your ticket or immediately afterwards, to purchase an exit row seat or a seat in the first row of the cabin that provides extra legroom.

Chapter 5

PLANNING AND PREPARATION

Philippians 4:19 (ASV)
"And my God will supply every need of yours according to his riches in glory in Christ Jesus."

To begin your mission in Uganda, both a U.S. passport and a Ugandan entry Visa are required to enter the country. For current information visit the United States Department of State website at https://travel.state.gov/content/travel/en/international-travel/International-Travel-Country-Information-Pages/Uganda.html.

Passport. As a visitor to Uganda from the United States, you will need an official passport that will not expire for at least six months beyond the date that you will complete your travel within the country. If you are applying for a U.S. passport for the first time or renewing your passport, visit the U.S. State Department website for information regarding the application process and pricing: https://travel.state.gov/content/travel/en/passports/apply-renew-passport/apply-in-person.html.

Visa. An entry Visa is required to enter Uganda. In years past, Ugandan entry Visas could be obtained upon arrival at the Entebbe Airport. This option is no longer available and since July 1, 2016, the Ugandan Government requires entry Visas to be obtained through an online application process at https://visas.immigration.go.ug/. In order to complete the online application process you will need to upload:

1. A copy of your yellow fever certification
2. A page from your valid passport
3. A recent passport sized photo of yourself

Although the website advises that the application process should be completed at least two weeks prior to your planned departure date, as an extra measure of caution, we suggest completing the process at least four weeks prior to departure.

Vaccinations and Medications

For the most up-to-date information regarding vaccinations for travel to Uganda, visit the Center for Disease Control websites at https://wwwnc.cdc.gov/travel/destinations/traveler/none/Uganda. For planning purposes below is a summary of the information as of January 2018.

Required: Since yellow fever is a risk in Uganda, the Yellow Fever vaccination is required for all travelers. The Customs and Immigration officer will ask you to present the yellow fever certification card as proof of vaccination before you will be permitted to enter into the country.

Recommended: The CDC recommends Typhoid and Hepatitis A vaccinations as both diseases may be contracted through contaminated food and water. CDC also recommends the Meningitis vaccine if you plan to visit Uganda during the dry season (December–June).

Recommended: To prevent against the risk of contracting malaria, the CDC recommends that travelers to Uganda take an anti-malaria prescription medication before, during and after your trip to Uganda.

Suggested: In addition to the medications mentioned above, the CDC suggests the Hepatitis B and Rabies vaccinations for some travelers.

Routine: The CDC encourages all travelers to make sure their routine vaccines are up-to-date before traveling to Uganda. These vaccines include measles-mumps-rubella (MMR) vaccine, diphtheria-tetanus-pertussis vaccine, varicella (chickenpox) vaccine, polio vaccine, and your yearly flu shot.

Fundraising

One of the most daunting parts of a calling to mission in Africa can be raising the funds needed for the trip. Fortunately, by searching "mission trip fundraising ideas" on Google, you will find several websites that provide great suggestions to help you choose and develop specific fundraisers. Some that worked well for our last mission team were silent auctions at church in which mission team members auctioned items and personal services, raffles of homemade wreaths and other decorative items for various holidays, and team garage sales.

The best approach is to send out a personal call to action to family, friends and fellow church members. The informational letter should share about the mission call you have received to Uganda, the work you will be doing and your need for both prayerful and financial support for the trip. Below is a sample letter that can be refined to meet your needs:

Dear _____:

Hello, how are you? I hope that you are doing well and that God is doing many wonderful things in your life. I am writing to share about a challenging ministry opportunity that He has presented to me. In 201_, God has offered me the opportunity to travel to Uganda, Africa, as part of a mission team with [Organization Name]. This ____ day mission trip will be focused on serving and sharing the gospel with orphans, vulnerable children and others who are sick or in need.

While God has opened up a door for me to serve and to share His heart of compassion for His people around the world, I would like to invite you to share in this journey of compassion along with me. First, you can help by praying for my fellow team members and myself. We will need prayers that God will prepare us for our visit and bless our efforts as we minister to the people of Uganda. We will also need prayers that our financial needs will be met. At this time we each need to raise $_____ for our travel and living expenses, and that is quite a challenge! I hope to raise the majority of my funds by [DATE] in order to pay for airline tickets and other items.

Another way you can be involved is to help provide financial support. Would you consider supporting me with a donation? I have included a postage-paid envelope for you to use if you feel led to contribute. Checks can be made payable to [non-profit organization]. You can learn more about [non-profit organization] at [website address] and may also make a donation through the [organiztion's] secure online donation site at [non-profit organization donation site]. When making an online donation, please include

Uganda Mission – *[insert missionary name]* in the provided description box. Any donation amount would allow you or your business to take a deduction for the 20__ tax year, as allowed by law. The [non-profit organization] TAX ID number is _____.

Thank you for being an important part of my life. Whether you feel led to contribute financially, through prayer, or both, all of your support is appreciated. I look forward to doing God's work in Uganda and sharing with you about how God has worked through this team after our trip. Please email me at _____ or call me at _____ if you have any questions or suggestions.

May God Bless You,

NAME
Address
Phone number
Email Address[9]

TIP: Report back to those who supported you financially and prayerfully. Take Mark 5:19-20 to heart, "...Go home and tell your friends what the Lord has done..."

42

Chapter 6

PACKING AND GIFT ITEMS

Luke 6:38 (NIV)
"Give, and it will be given to you. A good measure, pressed down, shaken together and running over, will be poured into your lap. For with the measure you use, it will be measured to you."

Short-term mission trips to Uganda often last between ten days to three weeks. Sometimes the length may be as short as seven days or extend for several months. You will want to adjust the suggested packing lists to fit your schedule and needs.

The most important guidance for this section is that while in Uganda, it is appropriate to follow the customs of the area in which you are visiting. Ugandans living in villages typically dress in more traditional attire than those living in cities. For example, women living in villages almost always wear long dresses or skirts while women living in cities may wear long skirts, knee length skirts or even pants. Similarly, though it would be almost unheard of to see a Ugandan man wearing shorts in a village, this might occur in the city (albeit still rarely). Regardless of where they live, Ugandans dress well for church and work and strive for cleanliness and neatness in their appearance.

SUGGESTED PACKING LIST

TIPS:
Airlines vary in the number of checked bags they allow for international flights to Africa so be sure to check the rules for your flight. Some airlines offer special "missionary" fares that include an additional bag at no extra charge.

✻✻✻

Be sure to pack at least one full change of clothing, appropriate for the activities planned for your first day in Uganda, in your carry-on bag along with any other critical toiletry items in case one or more of your checked bags are delayed in arrival.

Women:

For women, clothes should be modest and loose fitting. Dress casually except for when you are in church when you will want to be a little more dressed up. If worn at all, jewelry should be inexpensive.

- ☐ 1-2 pairs of jeans, or lightweight pants or capri's
- ☐ 3-5 skirts full length for Village
- ☐ 4-7 t-shirts for daily wear with skirts
- ☐ 1-2 dressier tops and skirts or dress for church
- ☐ 1-2 long sleeve shirts
- ☐ 1-2 Tank tops to wear on safari (not low cut,)
- ☐ 1-2 pairs of shorts to wear on safari
- ☐ 1 hoodie/sweatshirt
- ☐ 1 jacket/sweater
- ☐ Tennis shoes
- ☐ Sleepwear
- ☐ Swimsuit (modest)
- ☐ Flip flops or other shower shoes
- ☐ 5-7 underwear/bras/sports bras
- ☐ 2-3 socks
- ☐ Sports sandals
- ☐ Nice shoes/sandals for church
- ☐ 1 hat
- ☐ Headband, ponytail holders, hair clips

Men:

Clothes should be, modest, loose fitting and casual, except for when you are in church when you will want to more nicely attired.

- ☐ 3-4 pairs of jeans (one nice pair/one work pair)
- ☐ 3-4 pairs of khaki or longer shorts
- ☐ 1-2 nice polo's or button up shirts for church services
- ☐ 1-2 pairs of Slacks/Dockers for church
- ☐ T-shirts
- ☐ Swimming trunks
- ☐ 1 sweatshirt/jacket
- ☐ Sleepwear
- ☐ 3-5 socks
- ☐ 5-7 underwear
- ☐ Sports sandals
- ☐ Dressier shoes for church
- ☐ 1 hat for sun protection
- ☐ Tennis shoes
- ☐ Flip flops or other shower shoes

Personal Items

- ☐ 1 towel for use in villages
- ☐ 1 washcloth for use in villages

- ☐ Face wash
- ☐ Toothbrush and toothpaste
- ☐ Comb and/or brush
- ☐ Shampoo and conditioner
- ☐ Deodorant
- ☐ Lotion
- ☐ 1 to 2 rolls travel toilet tissue
- ☐ 1-2 large packages of baby wipes for use in the village if shower availability is limited
- ☐ Kleenex
- ☐ Soap
- ☐ Anti-bacterial hand sanitizer
- ☐ Finger nail file and clippers
- ☐ Razor
- ☐ Shaving cream
- ☐ Make-up
- ☐ Feminine hygiene products (Tampons are not available and pads are often difficult to find.)

Medicine

- ☐ Malaria pills
- ☐ Other prescription medications provided by your doctor (anti-bacterial, anti-nausea, anti-biotic, etc.)

- ☐ Medication from home (Vitamins, Tylenol, Ibuprofen, Flu/Congestion Medicine, Airborne, Neosporin, Bandaids, Etc.)

Documents

- ☐ Passport
- ☐ Copy of Passport (Keep separate location from original)
- ☐ Insurance cards or papers
- ☐ Vaccination Card and Yellow Fever Certification
- ☐ Copy of Vaccination Card and Yellow Fever Certification
- ☐ Doctor's note of any allergies, prescription medicine or any other physical conditions in case at visit to international clinic is needed.

Other Essentials

- ☐ Earplugs or noise canceling earphones are highly recommended for the trip to lessen the noise of crying babies on the flight, snoring seatmates, noisy vehicle engines, barking dogs, etc.
- ☐ Movies are offered on the long flights and your Bible, playing cards, a good book, or iPod all help pass the flight time.

☐ Money belt

TIP: This may not make you the coolest person in the city, but it can add an element of protection from would be pick pockets.

☐ Sunscreen
☐ Insect repellent (Strong/DEET)

TIP: We take the spray and lotion versions and for those of you who chose not to ignore my suggestion above, my favorite is the wipe version that fits in my...you guessed it...money belt.

☐ Mosquito repellant bracelet and anklet

TIP: I don't know if they really work but I think they work so I make sure we all wear them the entire time we are in the country and we rarely get mosquito bites while there.

☐ Anti-itch cream (in case you get mosquito bites)
☐ Aloe Vera
☐ Chap stick
☐ Sunglasses

- ☐ Umbrella
- ☐ Travel Rain Poncho
- ☐ Journal
- ☐ Daypack/Backpack (An absolute must)
- ☐ Bandanna or other face cover for dusty road trips

TIP: Don't forget to pack a face cover; if it's hot and dry and you are traveling in a van with a group, the windows will be open. The dust can be intense!

- ☐ Camera
- ☐ Cell phone (with international calling plan, wifi calling or if it can hold a SIM card)
- ☐ Small Flashlight or solar lantern

TIP: You may or may not need this, however, if you need it and you don't have it, you will really wish you did. On one of our trips, the "restroom" was several hundred feet away from where we slept and it was important to see where we were stepping on the way and once inside the roofless facility. Even if it isn't needed, it is a perfect departing gift to leave with a local mission staff member who made your trip special.

- ☐ IPAD/Tablet w/downloaded movies/books

- ☐ Bible
- ☐ Pens/Pencils
- ☐ Card games
- ☐ Over the shoulder small purse
- ☐ Travel first aid kit (one per family)

TIP: I take a small first aid kit that fits in my handy, dandy money belt.

- ☐ Travel size sewing kit
- ☐ Travel alarm clock
- ☐ Laundry detergent travel packet
- ☐ ATM card/Credit cards

TIP: MasterCard is not as widely accepted as VISA

- ☐ Treated mosquito net (precautionary)
- ☐ Sleeping bag or light blanket for Village (if suggested by your mission organization)
- ☐ Plug adapter/transformer/converter

TIP: In a nutshell, if using western electrical appliances you will need both a converter and an adapter. Having blown fuses in lodging establishments in Uganda and multiple countries (which can be very embarrassing, especially when half the guest house in a small German village goes dark and the only thing you understand from the loud German voices down the hall is "Americans!"), I admit that I don't really understand the technical details but highly suggest that you visit the following website for more information: https://www.adaptelec.com/index.php?main_page=advanced_search_result&search_in_description=1&zenid=1160ek40vkum1lqqothelbv6g4&keyword=Uganda

What about snacks?

Ugandans do not typically snack during the day but do enjoy trying some of the new treats you offer them from the U.S. In all honesty, we take many more snacks than we need but it is always easy to find someone (or many people) with whom to share. Many (if not all) of these items are typically included in our packed bags:

- ☐ Granola bars
- ☐ Pop Tarts

- ☐ Beef jerky
- ☐ Fruit chews
- ☐ Trail mix
- ☐ Chips
- ☐ Cookies
- ☐ Peanut butter or cheese crackers
- ☐ Wheat thins/Cheese Its
- ☐ Small packages of flat bread
- ☐ Small jars of peanut butter and jelly

<u>Snacks are great but what about my caffeine?</u>

It is easy to purchase soft drinks, hot tea or coffee for your morning caffeine if you are staying at a hotel or guesthouse in an urban area. Unfortunately, caffeine options may be limited to non-existent is some rural villages. My go to solution is to take tea bags and a clear plastic bottle that I can use to make sun tea. It brews naturally and quickly and as soon as I toss in a pre-packaged sweetener, I am good to go. So for those of you reading this section, add:

- ☐ Tea bags
- ☐ Clear plastic bottle
- ☐ Pre-packaged sweetener

☐ Instant coffee (hotels or guest houses often provide hot water)

Small Gift Items (Optional)

Please check with the mission organization with which you will be working to see if there will be an opportunity to share gifts items. Most organizations allow short-term missionaries to share small gift items though some do not. For Live in Light mission trips, our policy is to work alongside a local church or other local Christian organization for the distribution of clothing items, Bibles, eyeglasses or other more valuable items. We believe it is important for the children and community to recognize that the items are being made available through the local organization rather than a short-term ministry team. Although our team members may participate in the distribution process, it should be clear that the local organization is leading the effort.

We believe that is acceptable for ministry team members to share small inexpensive gifts with children (and adults if they would like one, and many are happy to receive them). Our favorite gift item is a brightly colored, plastic cross necklace (available for purchase on

Amazon.com and Oreintaltrading.com) that we give to boys and girls (adults also often appreciate them).

©2017 [11]

Other suggested items include pencils, pens, pencil sharpeners, small bouncy balls, paper airplane gliders (though from experience, if you go with the gliders, be prepared to be running around chasing them for hours), Christian stickers and bookmarks, plastic friendship bracelets and toy cars. Also from experience, bubble gum is a big hit but you have to make sure the recipient gives you the wrapper immediately after opening it, otherwise it will be tossed to the wind (literally) and you will be running around picking up bubble gum wrappers for hours. That is a lot of running around if you hand out gliders and bubble gum on the same day...just sayin'. If you do not see something on this list, check out Oriental trading and Amazon as both have a lot of great party favor/vacation bible school type items.

Chapter 7

HEALTH AND SAFETY

2 Timothy 1:7 (NLV)
"For God did not give us a spirit of fear. He gave us a spirit of power and of love and of a good mind."

Uganda is considered one of safest countries to visit in Africa. Visitors are encouraged to exercise the same caution while in Kampala, and other urban areas, as you would in a large city anywhere in the world. Take care to pay attention to your surroundings and keep money and other valuables out of sight. Do not go out alone. If you will be out after dark, make sure you have a local traveling companion or stay with a group in areas with which you are familiar as it is easy to become lost in new surroundings.

With little exception, I have rested in the comfort of God's calling and protection during our travels in Uganda. In full confession, however, some of the most alarming moments in my life occurred on our first trip to Africa. Because our flight arrived in Uganda late at night, we traveled to a nearby hotel so we could sleep for a few hours before continuing our journey to the organization's recently acquired property located near a rural village in the Luweero District. The next morning we excitedly boarded the van for an early morning departure. Our eyes were glued to the windows as we viewed the urban scenery, which was already full of people and cars competing busily to make their way through the traffic, and we loved seeing the children of all ages dressed in so many different hues of neatly washed uniforms already headed to their respective schoolhouses. The landscape continued to engage us as it became more rural during the ninety-minute van ride. We continued to see Ugandans, though not in throngs, and had to halt our progress on a couple of occasions to allow boys, who could not have been older than thirteen, to cajole long-horned cows out of the middle of the road. The last few miles of the journey required our van; overloaded with people and three days of camping supplies, to travel a "road" that really was not any such thing. At one point, a few of the amazing Ugandan staff climbed on the roof in hopes of getting a better view of the rough terrain.

If you have ever lived near or spent time camping by a river, you may be familiar with the two barely visible tire tracks that require vehicles to careen through ditches, avoid mud holes and sometimes cross a fallen log in order to reach the best fishing/swimming hole on the river that only the local's know about. That is exactly the type of passage we experienced on the last two miles of the trip to our destination, except that it was roughly carved out of the African wilderness and there was no fishing hole at the end.

Upon arrival, we realized that there were no buildings on the property, although a small area had been cleared and there was a timeworn community school on the adjacent property. The projects for our team over the next three days were to build a community "squatty" structure (a traditional hole in the ground toilet facility) out of mud bricks and an inexpensive cement mixture, and traditional goat pens, out of small tree poles and the red clay mud, for some of the local villagers. We were thrilled to have disembarked from the van and had been in the very rural community for only a few minutes when the staff members began assigning the first tasks. My then fourteen-year-old daughter, Kaylee, and I volunteered to fill jerry cans (large water jugs) at the local well, which was about a quarter of a mile back down the flora wrapped red dirt trail. (As we merrily departed, I happened to catch a glance of the look of angst on Mark's (my husband's) face when he realized that he was assigned to a different task and would not be going with us).

At the well, Kaylee and I cheerfully got in line with the many energetic, friendly children waiting to collect water for their families. The children were clearly wondering and chatting about us in the local language, as they had not seen us before. Everything was new to us so we probably had classic deer in the headlight looks as we tried to interact with them. It was soon our turn and a couple of sweet young boys demonstrated the motions required to pump the water, which required a bit of effort. After a few minutes, I turned to ask Kaylee if she was ready to give me a break. Engaging with children beside me only seconds before, she was now GONE.

I frantically and quickly looked around the well and did not see her. (Unlike Halley, my youngest, Kaylee was not the type of child to wander off; she may not admit it but she let me hold her hand in large parking lots until she was eleven.) Several small to medium sized African children surrounded me in every direction but there was no white, fourteen year old teen...ANYWHERE!!! I turned another complete circle (I remember it as if I was turning in slow motion) and expanded my view by a few feet. She was definitely not there. By now, the boys who had been helping me were figuring out that something was not quite right with this strange lady and began showing some looks of concern (perhaps for their own safety), but I didn't care because MY BABY HAD BEEN KIDNAPPED IN THE AFRICAN BUSH!!!! (I literally had that exact thought.)

One-half second before letting loose a piercing, "at the top of my lungs," panicked, scream (like I actually did once at a department store when she was three and I didn't see her playing in the middle of a circular clothes rack that I was browsing) I saw her. Headed back toward the camp, she was carrying a jerry can filed with water for the tiniest little girl, who looked to be about four years old and not much bigger than the water jug from which Kaylee had rescued her.

At that moment, I felt the presence of my God the Protector and was impressed with the peace of knowing that we were safe in Africa because He had called us there to serve. I have retained that sense of comfort whenever we are in Uganda and the picture I took (after my peace-filled moment) is one of my all-time favorites. The beautiful little girl, Sauda, rarely left Kaylee's side the entire time we were in the community and is now a sponsored child to our family.

14

Tips for Staying Healthy

Getting sick on mission is the last thing you, or anyone, wants. I can assure you on behalf of my family, that it is not a pleasant experience. Mercifully, we only experienced it on our first trip to Uganda in 2010, when a couple of us were hit with a stomach bug. Fortunately, we had anti-nausea medication that our doctor had prescribed so the effects were not long lasting.

Below are a few suggestions that may help you avoid it altogether:

- Only drink bottled water or water that you are sure has been purified and filtered.

- Stay hydrated. Even if the organization you are working with provides bottled water, it is a good idea to carry a couple of extra of your own just in case supplies run short.

- Do not purchase food from local street vendors or restaurants that do not appear to meet sanitation standards

- Unless you are certain that offered fruits and vegetables have been washed with purified water, stick with options that you can personally wash or peel.

- Carry a small bottle of sanitizer with you at all times and apply frequently. Ugandan children will love holding your hand, arm, or leg (unless they can convince you to pick them up).

- Avoid touching your face or mouth while on assignment.

- Let properly covered experts help anyone who is bleeding or vomiting

- Use a straw to drink from a soft-drink bottle because the bottles are re-used.

- Always wear insect repellant and sunscreen.

- Provide a traveling companion with a completed medical consent form identifying any special medical conditions or allergies you may have.

- GET YOUR VACCINATIONS.

- TAKE YOUR ANTI-MALARIA MEDICATION. EVERY DAY. There are several options so make sure you discuss with your doctor.

- Take other medications (anti-nausea, traveler's diarrhea, Imodium AD, anti-biotic, anti-bacteria, etc., with you when you travel overnight to new locations).

Medical Care

If you do become ill, there are several good international hospitals and medical clinics in Kampala and other cities. Medical treatment is generally less expensive than in the U.S. but typically requires cash payment.

Chapter 8

ARRIVAL AND TRANSPORTATION

Matthew 5:14-16 (MSG)
"You're here to be light, bringing out the God-colors in the world. God is not a secret to be kept. We're going public with this, as public as a city on a hill. If I make you light-bearers, you don't think I'm going to hide you under a bucket, do you? I'm putting you on a light stand. Now that I've put you there on a hilltop, on a light stand—shine! Keep open house; be generous with your lives. By opening up to others, you'll prompt people to open up with God, this generous Father in heaven."

The international airport of Uganda is located in the town of Entebbe, on the shores of Lake Victoria, approximately twenty miles from Kampala City. Despite the short distance, travel times between Entebbe and Kampala can vary greatly depending upon traffic. Our trips have ranged from a quick forty minutes after a midnight arrival to three hours during a mid-day traffic jam so always plan more time than you expect to need.

The airport is about the size of a nice regional airport in the U.S. and consists of one terminal for international flights and a second for domestic flights. The airport is not hard to navigate and after exiting the plane, you will easily be able to follow the crowd down a long hallway to the customs and immigration area where signs will direct you to the appropriate entry line. Be prepared for some customs lines to move quickly while others progress slowly. If you choose a slowly moving line, enjoy visual exploration of your surroundings while you wait your turn. Customs agents are not overly friendly but neither are they rude. Agents will typically ask your purpose for being in the country and since you will technically be entering the country on an ordinary/tourism visa, the easiest answer seems to be tourist. Just be prepared to answer more questions if you choose to share more purpose related details. Agents may also ask where you will be staying while in the country. Since many mission teams travel to a few locations while in the country, you can just provide the address of a primary location at which you will be staying. Most importantly, have your passport, visa documentation, and immunization and yellow fever cards ready when you approach the agent booth and it should proceed smoothly. If you are traveling as a family, it is fine to approach the agent booth together.

Luggage Collection and Missing Bags

Once you have cleared customs you will proceed to the luggage pickup area. Bags arrive reasonably soon on conveyor belts. If you are like us, you will have several bags and will need a push cart to help transport them to your vehicle so go ahead and grab one before you start pulling your bags off the belt. If one, or more, of your bags does not arrive when you do, ask an airport employee to direct you to the lost luggage desk where you will be able to complete a form and provide a description of your missing item. We have arrived with all of our bags on two of our four trips, so it is probably safe to assume fifty-fifty odds that all of your luggage will make it. The airport authorities do a good job of locating and delivering missing bags. On both occasions, our bags were delivered to our hotel within twenty-four hours after our arrival.

TIP: On our last trip, we carried photos of our bags, which made it much easier to describe our missing luggage during the "missing bag description" discussion.

Exchanging Money for Shillings

If you are uncertain as to when you will have a chance to visit an ATM in Uganda, it is a good idea to stop by one of the currency exchange booths, located near the luggage conveyor belts, to exchange your Western currency for Ugandan Shillings. The agents are usually very friendly and happy to explain the exchange process if you have any questions. We typically exchange about $50 in the airport and then make ATM withdrawals as needed during our stay. Since ATM's charge local processing and foreign exchange fees in addition to fees that may be assessed by your bank, it is important to check ATM withdrawal policies for foreign travel before you leave the U.S.

TIP: Most banks, exchange bureaus and shops in Uganda refuse to accept older U.S. bills so make sure the bills you take with you are not dated prior to 2005.

Exiting the Airport

Interestingly, you may be required to put your bags through a luggage scan device before departing the secured airport area. This was a new step in the process during our trip in March and I was quite confused as to the purpose. Apparently, the agent working the scanner was not sure either. Although there was a line forming at the scanner, when he saw our group of thirteen, each with two large checked bags and two carry-ons, he just waived us around the line and out the door. As you exit the airport, do not be surprised if there is a large group of taxi or passenger service providers vying for your attention in hopes of gaining a fare. At times, it can be a bustling and noisy atmosphere.

Ground Transportation

Pre-arranging ground transportation from the airport to your destination, through your mission organization or a car service, should help with initial cultural adjustment. Every time we leave the secured area of the airport, I can't help but remember the moments of confusion we experienced on our first trip when we unknowingly walked into the throng of transport vendors. Perplexity was quickly followed by a feeling of confidence upon seeing a friendly face just above a sign with our names on it.

Recently, "Sue", the friend of an acquaintance, contacted me. Sue and a group of fellow retirees were planning their first mission trip to Uganda and wanted to confirm with me that the yellow fever vaccination was required to enter the country. At the time, I was sitting at the gas station having just filled up my car. My daughter, Halley, was with me and since it was a warm day, she handed me a cold water bottle she had just purchased. After responding to the yellow fever question, I took a drink from the water bottle just as Sue asked another question, "We are hoping to rent a van to drive while we are in Uganda, will that be okay and easy to do at the airport?" Surprised by her question, my quick air intake caused me to choke on the water. After subduing the full on choking/coughing reflex, and ignoring Halley's raised eyebrows, I tried to recover gracefully and responded respectfully but firmly, "No, no ma'am that really is not a good idea."

Road travel in Uganda can be a bit overwhelming, especially in Kampala. There are a limited number of traffic signals in the city and frequently, you will find yourself in four, or even five, lanes of traffic competing for space in an area that was built for two. I seriously cannot count the number of times that I was one hundred percent convinced that we were about to hit, or be hit by, at least one other vehicle and then to my complete surprise, the certain accident was completely avoided. For American drivers, it seems like absolute mayhem; Ugandan drivers are well trained and successfully traverse the seemingly impossible routes like seasoned pros. You absolutely do not want to drive yourself on your first short-term mission trip to Uganda.

TIP: For your first visit, leave driving in Uganda to the local experts.

Fortunately, you can hire a car service with a driver at very reasonable rates. In addition to car rental companies, many of the safari companies also offer daily car service and rates. Be sure to check reviews on TripAdvisor.com if you are in charge of making the car service selection. If you would like a personal suggestion, feel free to email me at *info@liveinlightministries.org*. I will be happy to make introductions to a couple of companies that I know well and trust to help you make arrangements for car service, accommodation or safari arrangements if needed.

"Matatus" and "boda bodas" are other common modes of transport in Uganda. Matatus, also referred to as taxis, are commercial passenger vans, often white with blue stripes, that allow passengers to get on and off along a specific route. Although, the vans typically have fourteen seats, the number of passengers allowed to ride on any given route can and will be much higher than fourteen. I have frequently heard, "Taxi drivers have never seen a passenger that wouldn't fit." Boda Bodas are motorcycle taxis that are also very common in Uganda. Drivers often carry as many as three passengers on one boda boda, though sometimes you may see a driver with one passenger and a large piece of furniture. You honestly just never know what might be coming around the next corner. Although many short-term missionaries have safely ridden on boda bodas, we have seen more than enough accidents (or almost accidents that were too close for comfort) to strongly advise our Live in Light mission team members against doing so.

TIP: As a former English territory, Uganda follows the left side driving rules so be sure to double check oncoming traffic before crossing the road as a pedestrian.

Chapter 9

FOOD AND LODGING

Matthew 25:35-40 (NIV)
"For I was hungry and you gave me something to eat, I was thirsty and you gave me something to drink, I was a stranger and you invited me in, I needed clothes and you clothed me, I was sick and you looked after me, I was in prison and you came to visit me. Then the righteous will answer him, 'Lord, when did we see you hungry and feed you, or thirsty and give you something to drink? When did we see you a stranger and invite you in, or needing clothes and clothe you? When did we see you sick or in prison and go to visit you?' The King will reply, 'Truly I tell you, whatever you did for one of the least of these brothers and sisters of mine, you did for me.'"

Over half of the men, women and children in Uganda lack access to safe drinking water.[18] While traveling in Uganda, Americans should assume that water from any tap, well, or other local source, is contaminated and should only drink water from a bottle with a sealed lid. While most mission organizations provide bottled water for daily consumption, out of an abundance of caution and a few experiences when group supplies ran short, we advise our mission team members to take advantage of opportunities to purchase and carry a couple of extra bottles.

TIP: Don't forget to use bottled or treated water when brushing and rinsing your teeth.

Coffee and tea are available at many restaurants that meet western sanitation standards. Just follow the rule of care and if in doubt, stick with the bottled water or soda.

The food in Uganda is quite yummy. Breakfast is offered at many hotels and guesthouses in the city and usually includes toast, fresh fruit, tea and juice. Sometimes, other items like egg or sausage are served. Breakfast in the Village usually consists of toast and/or eggs. Expect most midday meals to include a variation of beans and rice, along with a local favorite such as matooke (a boiled plantain) or posho (a boiled cornmeal mix).

Depending upon whether you are in the city or a rural village, evening meals in Uganda may range from basic American meals, such spaghetti and meat sauce, to a traditional Ugandan meal, which may include meat sauce, sausages, or beans mixed and fried with vegetables poured over rice or potatoes, and greens. On the best nights, the meal will include chapatti bread, which is like a thin tortilla but ten times better.

Lodging and Amenities in the City

There are many secure, "westernized" budget accommodations for short-term missionaries in Kampala. Please note that cleanliness standards and the quality of mosquito nets provided by budget hotels vary greatly in Uganda. Be sure to check guest reviews on TripAdvisor.com for hotels close to the area in which you will be working.

Even though it is becoming more westernized, Kampala and its establishments still experience power and water outages on occasion. We have experienced at least one outage on each of our previous trips, including one water outage that lasted for two days. Even when there is not an outage, the water source is often unreliable. Sometimes the water pressure is good; sometimes it is a trickle. Sometimes the water will be warm; often it is cold. Unfortunately, we have not been able to figure out a time of day that is better than other times.

TIP: Baby wipes come in handy when staying in a rural village with limited shower options and in the city if the water is out for a couple of days.

It is customary for travelers to drop their room keys at the front desk when leaving the hotel for the day. Although we have not had any problems, I have heard stories of travelers returning at the end of the day to find personal items missing. It is better to be safe by leaving any true valuables at home.

TIP: Passports, medicines and other important items should be left in a safe or carried with you.

Most hotels and guesthouses offer options for washing clothes onsite or at a nearby Laundromat. If you are on a tight schedule with little time to do laundry, many housekeepers offer laundry services for a small fee. They genuinely appreciate the opportunity to add extra income but in all fairness, I have found that they charge less than I am willing to pay so you may want to pay more than the requested amount. Another reliable method that has worked for us is to take a few travel packets of detergent so you can hand wash and hang critical items to dry in a window or restroom.

Lodging and Amenities in Rural Villages

If you will be spending nights in a rural village, it is likely that limited or no electricity will be available for at least part, if not all, of the time you are there. It is also very likely that flushing toilets will not be available. Accommodations may include a mattress on the floor of a guesthouse. We stayed in pop tents during our first two trips to Africa and to this day talk about the brilliancy of the stars that shown in the warm African bush. Though mosquito nets are often available even in rural villages, I recommend that our Live in Light mission team members bring one along with a light travel blanket just in case.

TIP: *We take the* **Lewis N. Clark travel comfort set** *that has a blow up pillow, which converts to a carry case, and a light blanket for use in villages.*

As mentioned previously, in most rural villages there is no running water. If there is not an overhead cistern system, a cup and bucket of water may be provided for your shower. Shower stalls are usually an outside mud brick enclosure that may or may not have a roof. Warm water is not usually available. Baby wipes are very nice to have in the Village.

Below is an excerpt from Kaylee's blog during our last trip to the rural village that we visit in Uganda.

Today was our first day back in the village and wow, was it spectacular?!! I love everything about this place from the smiling babies to the peaceful elders. The village is holy ground and you can feel God's presence the moment you step out of the van..."When God has blessed you, you then must bless others." I heard that statement this morning during the church service in the village, and have not stopped thinking about it. Of course, we hear some form of this all the time, how it is important to help others when they have less. But for some reason, God made sure I heard it spoken in this way and it worked. I am insanely, amazingly, and crazily blessed, and I must do everything in my power to provide to those who have less. Those ten words have opened my eyes with a whole new perspective and I am thankful.

Chapter 10

COMMUNICATING WITH FRIENDS AND FAMILY IN THE STATES

Luke 18:29-30 (MSG)
"Yes," said Jesus, "and you won't regret it. No one who has left home, spouse, brothers and sisters, parents, children—whatever—will lose out. It will all come back multiplied many times over in your lifetime..."

One of the questions I'm asked most frequently by future mission team members is how they will communicate with family and friends while in Uganda. The two primary ways are by cell phone and Internet. While in the city, there are usually opportunities to phone home each day, unless for some reason the Internet or cellular service is temporarily down. Unfortunately, contacting friends and family members from rural villages is much less reliable unless you are able to pick up a local cell tower so that you can send a text message or perhaps even connect or a call. Live in Light mission team members are encouraged to let friends and family members know when they will be traveling to a village and that they should not expect hear from them for a few days.

Cell Phone

In order to avoid excessive roaming charges, check with your telephone service carrier for international calling/text plans. We typically add the ATT Passport plan (one-time charge) which includes unlimited text and limited calling for one family phone and use the hotel Wi-Fi for our other phones. If you have an unlocked cell phone that has a SIM card, or purchase an inexpensive one, it is possible to buy a Ugandan network SIM card and local airtime for just few dollars. Friends and family can call you on this phone and it will be no charge to you but subject to fee associated with their international calling plans. You can also purchase a local phone with sim card from one of the Ugandan mobile providers for $15 to $20. Just be sure to plan a stop at one of the many mobile providers (they are literally everywhere) shortly after arriving in the country to make your purchases so friends and family back home will not be worrying unnecessarily.

Internet

Internet service in Uganda is not the same as in the States, so have patience and flexibility regarding its reliability. Many hotels and guesthouses offer free Wi-Fi. Usually, the best reception is in the lobby (or if you are fortunate to get a room close to the lobby). Even in the lobbies of most hotels we have stayed at, coverage is spotty and connections may be down for several hours. When it is working, if you do not mind visiting with friends or family members from the lobby, Skype, Facebook calling, Google Hangout and other apps can usually be used for free wifi calls with or without the video option.

TIP: If you have not used wifi or video calling before, it would be best to set up your accounts so you can practice using the different apps before leaving the US.

Chapter 11

COMMUNICATING IN UGANDA

Matthew 25:40 *(NIV)*
"The King will reply, 'Truly I tell you, whatever you did for one of the least of these brothers and sisters of mine, you did for me.'

Following its British colonial years, Uganda retained English as the official national language. Most educated Ugandans, shopkeepers and civil service workers are fluent in English; and in our experience, most hotel employees, taxi drivers and others living and working in urban areas speak enough English to permit communication. Road and retail signs are also in English, so it is not too difficult for Western visitors to travel throughout the country.

As you journey into more rural areas, you are likely to encounter adults, and some children who are unable to afford school fees, who do not speak English. Although more than forty different local languages are spoken in the country, two native languages commonly encountered by foreign visitors are Swahili and Luganda. Swahili was added in 2005 as a regionally important second official language of Uganda but it is primarily spoken in areas located near the border with Kenya. Luganda is considered the most geographically widespread language and you will hear it spoken frequently when touring both cities and villages.

Language APPs and Helpful Words and Phrases

If you speak English and can learn a few greetings or words from the Luganda word guide below, you should be well on your way to enjoying engaging conversations while in Uganda. For a more extensive list of words and phrases, search the Internet for "Luganda phrasebook" to find several good options, such as, the Peace Corps PDF document.[23] If you want to become even more conversant, Utalk offers Lugandan language apps that are generally useful. The *Utalk Classic - Learn Luganda* app is available inexpensively through the Apple App store. For expanded options *Go Talk – Learn Languages* is also offered by Utalk and allows purchasers to choose from different categories at escalating rates. Both apps include helpful memory game and practice tools but I tend to use the classic version most frequently to brush up on commonly used greetings and words before each trip. If you prefer a free option, there are some good video options available on YouTube but without the memory game tools.

TIP: Try inexpensive Luganda language apps to learn words, phrases and correct pronunciations.

FIRST WORDS - LUGANDA LANGUAGE GUIDE

Common Words

English	Luganda	Pronunciation
Yes	Yee	(Yay)
No	Neda	(Nay-da)
Okay	Kale	(Call-ee)
Slowly	Mpola	(Mm-pole-la)
Sorry	Sonyiwa	Sone-e-wah)
Come	Jangu	(Ja-n-goo)
Left	Kono	(Ko-no)
Right	Dyo	(De-yo)

Useful Phrases

English	Luganda	Pronunciation
How are you?	Olyotia	(O-lee-o-tee-ya)
Fine	Gyendi	(Jen-dee)
I don't understand	Si te gala	(See-tee-ga-la)
How much?	Meka	(May-kah)
Please	Bambi	(Bom-be)
What time is it?	Sawa meka	(Saw-wah may-kah)

Thank you	Webale	(Way-ba-lee)
Thank you very much	Webale Nnyo	(Way-ba-lee N-yo)
Good	Bulungi	(Be-loon-gee)
Bad	Bubi	(Boob-e)
I am [name]	Nze [name]	(N-zee [name])
Who are you madam/sir?	Ggwe ani, nnyabo/ssebo?	(Ga-wanee nn-yah-bo/say-bo?)
Good afternoon	Wasibye otya	(Wa-see-be-o-te-ya)
Good night	Sula bulungi	(Su-la Be-loon-ge)
I am from America	Enva America	(N-va-wa America)
Let's go	Tugende	(To-gen-day)
Good-bye	Weeraba	(Wear-a-ba)
Welcome back	Kulikayo	(Ka-leak-i-oh)
I'm tired	Nkoye	(N-co-yea)
Speak slowly	Yogera mpola mpola	(Yo-ger-ra mm-pole-la mm-pole-la)
I want /need	Nja Gala	(N-jaw-ga-la)

Jesus Christ	Yesu Kristo	(Ye-sue Chris-toe)
Praise God	Mukama Yebazibwe	(Moo-ka-ma Ye-way-z-ba)
God loves you	Mukama Akwagala	(Moo-ka-ma A-kwa-ga-la)

People

English	**Luganda**	**Pronunciation**
Sir	Ssebo	(Say-bo)
Madam	Nnyabo	(nn-yah-bo)
Friend	Mukwano	(Moo-kwan-o)
Grandmother/Older Lady	Jaja	(Jah-jah)
Grandfather/Older man	Muzeyi	(Moo-za)

Food

English	**Luganda**	**Pronunciation**
Food	Emeere	(E-mary)
Rice	Mucere	(Moo-chair-e)
Beans	Ebijanjalo	(E-be-ja-nja-low)

Bananas	Amenvu	(A-men-voo)
Water	Amaazzi	(A-maaz-zee)
Coffee	Kaawa	(Kah-wa)
Tea	Chai	(ch-ai)
Sugar	Sukali	(Sue-call-e)
Salt	Munyo	(Moon-yo)

Nonverbal and Potentially Confusing Communications

Ugandans frequently use facial expressions to communicate. My favorite mission activity while in Uganda is working in an eyeglass clinic to serve adults in need of reading glasses. Bar none, the greatest joy of my trip is hearing the excitement of an elderly Ugandan who has just been fitted with the perfect strength lens. Though the days are long and physically exhausting as we each may help fit between fifty to seventy-five rural villagers in a day, I never tire of hearing the exclamation of delight that occurs when the words of the Lugandan Bible become perfectly clear for the recipient for first time in years, sometimes, even decades. Getting to that point of enthusiasm and finding the perfect lens; however, is a process that involves repeatedly inquiring whether the strength of the current lens is better than the previous one.

It took me a while to figure out that my questions were not being ignored but that I needed to step back to see if there was a non-verbal response. In response to a yes or no question, it is not uncommon for Ugandans to provide a "yes" response by raising their eyebrows, which may or not be accompanied by a sound best verbalized as "mmmmmm" through un-parted lips. Consider yourself forewarned that the "raised brow yes" can be an easy habit to acquire during your travels. Many times, we have returned to the United States and caught ourselves responding to bewildered friends and family members in such a manner.

Incidentally, in my eye clinic work, I also learned that Ugandan's are very polite. If a non-verbal cue was not presented, then the answer was no, the current lens was not better. In which case, I would ask if the last example was better which typically resulted in confirmation through a pair of emphatically raised brows in response. This leads to another important cultural communication point.

In my experience, many Ugandans do not want to disappoint others. Rather than provide a no answer to a suggestion or question, they may take a more optimistic view that the desired outcome, though unlikely, is technically possible and often answer affirmatively to a question when the answer should probably be no. We have experienced this several times, most recently when planning a two-day mini safari. When scheduling for our team, I inquired as to whether it would be possible to add a stop at the Rhino sanctuary on our return route to Kampala. The local booking agent assured me that the Rhino stop was "definitely possible and okay." Despite our full itinerary, I happily accepted the agent's confident assurances and added it to the schedule. In reality, however, with the morning game drive and afternoon lunch, it became clear that we would have arrived at the sanctuary after 5:00 p.m., less than an hour before closing time, with little chance of seeing the rhinos.

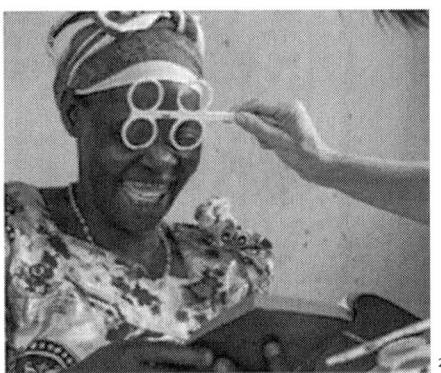

Chapter 12

ALL ABOUT FLEXIBILITY AND PATIENCE

Hebrews 10:36 (KJV)
"For ye have need of patience, that, after ye have done the will of God, ye might receive the promise."

Believed to be one of the greatest missionaries of all time, Hudson Taylor, founder of the China Inland Mission, is often quoted for having advised that "[t]here are three indispensable requirements for missionaries: 1) patience 2) patience 3) patience." This is definitely true for mission trips to Africa. There is much that could be said in this section, but sometimes less is more.

The culture and people will be very different.

> *Remember that you are a foreigner in a wonderful land of amazing people. Make it your goal to build long-term relationships. Ask their names and inquire about their lives. Be friendly, trusting and genuine.*

You will see things that do not make sense to you and will probably have suggestions on how some things could be done differently, or dare say even better.

> *Remember that unless specifically asked for input regarding a process, you are there to listen and serve without judgment. Be calm, cooperative and open to new ways of doing things.*

You may see degrees of poverty and pain that you never imagined possible.

> *Remember that Jesus is the one and only Savior and that your role is to serve those you can and to support the work being done. Show that you care.*

Schedules and times in Africa are always TENTATIVE. They can and often will change on a daily or even hourly basis. A planned 8:00 a.m. departure or start time may occur at 10:00 a.m. or later.

Remember that you are on God's schedule while in Africa. Every time the schedule changes, you have the opportunity to experience a new part of His plan. Be flexible and have patience.

TIP: Everything in Africa is **Tentative**. Programs and times can AND WILL change depending on AFRICA TIME.

25

Chapter 13

FREE TIME, TO SAFARI OR NOT TO SAFARI

Galatians 6:9 (NIV)
"*Let us not become weary in doing good, for at the proper time we will reap a harvest if we do not give up.*"

Those planning their first mission trips to Uganda, often ask (1) how they should spend their free time while in Uganda, and (2) whether they should go on Safari. As you might suspect, the answers to those questions are highly subjective depending upon personal interests, how much money you want to spend and the amount of time available. Regardless of what you choose, it is important to spend time resting and reflecting while on mission so that you do not become overly tired or weary. The good news is that there are many fun and interesting things to do in Uganda even if you have both limited time and budget.

To Safari or Not to Safari (2-3 days)

Starting with the question, whether to safari or not to safari, in all candidness, we chose not to go on safari our first two trips to Uganda because we did not want to take time away from our mission activities. After much encouragement from trusted team members, we decided to go on a two-day mini safari to Murchison Falls during our third visit and did not regret it. We now highly recommend the mini safari if you have the money, time and think your mission trip to Uganda will be a once in a lifetime experience.

Uganda has ten beautiful national parks from which to choose. For more information about the national parks, check out www.ugandasafariparks.com. We typically coordinate safari transportation and accommodation for our *Live in Light* mission teams directly with a safari company and you can do the same by following the process below:

(1) Determine the days that you plan to be on safari and the number of travelers in your party.

(2) Search for safari options offered during your desired dates and request quotes from several safari operators through an online search platform such as safaribookings.com. (The website limits the number of quotes you can request over a certain period, but I generally try to get at least five). Do not worry if the sample schedules that show up based on your search do not seem to match your desired itinerary. Just look for safari companies that offer schedules similar to what you want (e.g. two or three days to your desired park) at a reasonable cost. In my experience, you can customize your quote request based on your preferred dates and plans and the safari companies will respond with a quote to match your request. Do be sure to specify in your request for quotes whether you would like budget (typically a tent like structure), moderate (a comfortable safari hotel) or luxury (a very nice safari hotel) accommodation. We have not yet tried the tent option but have enjoyed our stays and were very comfortable in both moderate and luxury safari hotels.

(3) Compare the quotes you receive and ask any clarifying questions you may have from the companies that submitted the top proposals, including information about payment terms, pickup and drop off times and locations, type of vehicle etc. Depending upon the time of the year, I generally receive quotes ranging from $350 to $500 for two-day mini safaris with transport from Kampala to Murchison falls, including lodging, three or four meals and bottled water.

TIP: Although many companies ask for payment in full upon booking, if you ask, you may be able to put down a much lower deposit and pay the balance upon departure in Uganda.

---

(4) Before making a final selection, check the ratings for the companies that submitted the top proposals on TripAdvisor.com. There are many good options available so don't consider any company that does not have at least a 4.5 rating out of a possible of five.

If you want to go on safari but are not comfortable selecting a safari company, that is not a problem. You also have the option of working with a local travel service company that will help coordinate your safari schedule and any other travel, transportation or hotel needs you may have while in Uganda. The cost will be a bit higher, but it will alleviate some of your research and selection responsibilities. Another benefit is that these companies often send one of their staff on the trip to make sure everything goes as planned. If you would like some suggestions for a couple of these companies that I know well and trust, send me an email at *info@liveinlightministries.org* and I will be happy to make introductions.

Rhino Trekking (1 day)

For a wonderful day trip, consider the Ziwa Rhino and Wildlife Ranch located in Nakasongola district, approximately 100 miles north of Kampala. The Rhino re-introduction project is a collaboration of the Rhino Fund Uganda and Uganda Wildlife Authority and provides protection for the remaining wild rhinos in Uganda. For less than $50 per adult, and about half that for children, the sanctuary offers rhino trekking, bird watching and nature walks.

Entebbe Wildlife Education Center and Ngamba Island Chimpanzee Sanctuary (1/2 to 1 day)

If you do not have quite have a full day, but still want to see some of the native animal life, both the Entebbe Zoo and the Ngamba Chimpanzee Sanctuary offer excellent half or full day options near Entebbe. The Zoo charges low entry fees of $15 per person for foreign non-residents.

TIP: A word of caution for those of you who are captivated by the 'adorable' little monkeys roaming freely throughout the zoo. Yes, they are very cute but some are sneaky little guys just waiting for you to open or put down your bag to capture them in a picture. I promise, I'm an animal lover, but those little guys can scare the daylights out of you when they swoop in and try to grab something from your open bag, notwithstanding the fact that your family finds your frightful situation to be totally hilarious. Consider yourself warned....

27

The boat ride to Ngamba Island and the chimpanzee experience can be purchased from around $70 to $100 per person depending upon the number in your party and the type of boating experience you select. We have enjoyed visiting the animals before heading to the airport for late night flights back to the United States.

TIP: If you have a late night flight departing Uganda but don't want to get stuck in the late afternoon/evening traffic out of Kampala, the Entebbe Wildlife Education Center and the Ngamba Island Chimpanzee Sanctuary offer interesting and enjoyable options to see native animals in Entebbe.

Ndere Cultural Center and Dinner (Approximately 3 hours)

One of our favorite evening respites is the beautiful dinner performance currently offered on Wednesday, Friday and Sunday evenings at the Ndere Cultural in Kampala. For approximately $30, you can enjoy the outdoor dinner buffet and show, which expresses rich tribal differences through traditional dance, music, art and crafts. You may also watch the show for $15 without purchasing a dinner ticket. The event provides an entertaining and informative evening that will be enjoyed by mission team members of all ages. Although we have been (more than once) it is always anticipated as a highlight of future trips.

Craft Market (1 to 3.... 4, 5 hours)

Consider African crafts, jewelry or traditional clothing items for yourself or as gifts for friends and family. We have found wonderful craft markets throughout the country, so check with your mission organization to determine which local market options are closest to your mission field. Very nice crafts typically cost from $10 to $25 per item and small items are can cost between $2 to $5. Many Ugandan craft markets are set up in a way that leads shoppers through twists and turns between rows of shops. The retail craft booths often look very similar which makes it easy to get turned around, so pay careful attention to surroundings and visit shops that are within eyesight of a major access point or road.

TIP: If your group disperses at the craft market, set ground rules requiring everyone to stay in groups of three or more while shopping and agree upon a set departure time.

Chapter 14

REWINDING, REFLECTING AND RETURNING HOME

Matthew 5:13-15 (NLV)
"You are the salt of the earth. If salt loses its taste, how can it be made to taste like salt again? It is no good. It is thrown away and people walk on it."

It is my prayer that God will work through you to positively impact the lives of others on your mission trip, and that your life will also be changed for the better. As you near the end of your trip, you will likely experience many feelings, including sadness or loss. It is important to prepare for these emotions by participating in regular "debrief" sessions throughout your stay and ensure that you have a plan to continue them after your trip.

We have found it helpful for Live in Light mission teams to participate in rewind and reflection discussions at the end of each day, often during an evening worship time. Hearing team members share a "God moment," a touching experience, cultural insight or personal blessing that occurred during the day, often helps participants process their own experiences and builds deeper team connections. I also encourage you to record your personal God moments in a journal or daily calendar each night before you go to sleep. Review and reflect upon them as part of your morning prayer time before starting your day.

Just as you may have experienced culture shock upon arriving in Uganda, it is very common and normal to experience reverse culture shock upon returning home. God will have used the mission opportunity to open your eyes to a broader experience and it is important to continue the rewind and reflect process after your homecoming. Some team members have feelings of shock or even guilt when returning home and may find it challenging to share experiences with those who have not had a similar experience. Schedule at least one (but more if possible) group reflection process with your mission team members to discuss how God is working in and through you because of the mission work.

TIP: Love, learn, laugh and live in light while you are on mission then, upon return take time to rewind and reflect on what you experienced and accomplished, and the wonderful friendships you made while in Uganda.

END NOTES

[1] Washing the hands of younger relatives before eating in rural Uganda.

[2] Churchill, William. *My African Journey*. (London: Hodder & Stoughton, 1908).

[3] Baby boy's tears in a city orphanage.

[4] Photo credit http://gabisworld.com/data_images/countries/uganda/uganda-04.jpg

[5] Children in rural Luweero District.

[6] https://www.ugfacts.com/religion-in-uganda/

[7] http://www.who.int/countries/uga/en/

[8] http://www.worldatlas.com/articles/the-youngest-populations-in-the-world.html

[9] Live in Light Ministries sample mission fundraising support letter.

[10] Children attending school in a slum area in Kampala.

[11] Our favorite gift for children, a plastic cross necklace available on Amazon.com and OrientalTrading.com

[12] Sauda's brothers wearing their cross necklaces.

[13] The last mile on our first visit to a rural village in the Luweero District.

[14] Kaylee carrying Sauda's water jug on first meeting in 2010.

[15] Young girl carrying water jug in village in Luweero District.

[16] Photo credit http://www.kampalacitytour.com/wp-content/uploads/2015/03/kampala-traffic-during-peak-hours.jpg

[17] Boda Boda (motorcycle taxi) pickup location.

[18] https://www.water.org/our-impact/uganda/

[19] Traditional Ugandan meal in the village.

[20] Village family with new solar lantern for studying at night.

[21] Worship service in the beautiful church, built in 2012, in the rural community we visit.

[22] Showing Mountain and Uganda Telecom mobile service providers.

[23] http://files.peacecorps.gov/multimedia/audio/languagelessons/uganda/UG_Luganda_Language_Lessons.PDF

[24] "Mula Bulungi" the lens strength tried at the eye clinic is "very good!"

[25] Boy playing traditional drum in rural Luweero District.

[26] Elephant photo from mini-safari in Murchison Falls National Park.

[27] Sweet looking (but crazy) monkey at the Entebbe zoo will try to grab things from your bag while your family laughs.

[28] Traditional tribal dance at Ndere Cultural Center in Kampala.

[29] Children in rural Uganda enjoying previously loved stuffed animals shared by a mission team.

Made in the USA
Middletown, DE
16 May 2019